Skills Builders

YEAR 5

GRAMMAR, PUNCTUATION, SPELLING AND VOCABULARY TEACHER'S GUIDE

Sarah Turner

RISING ★ STARS

Although every effort has been made to ensure that website addresses are correct at time of going to press, Rising Stars cannot be held responsible for the content of any website mentioned in this book. It is sometimes possible to find a relocated web page by typing in the address of the home page for a website in the URL window of your browser.

Hachette UK's policy is to use papers that are natural, renewable and recyclable products and made from wood grown in sustainable forests. The logging and manufacturing processes are expected to conform to the environmental regulations of the country of origin.

ISBN: 978-1-78339-724-2

Text, design and layout © 2016 Rising Stars UK Ltd

First published in 2016 by Rising Stars UK Ltd
Rising Stars UK Ltd, An Hachette UK Company
Carmelite House, 50 Victoria Embankment
London, EC4Y 0DZ

www.risingstars-uk.com

All facts are correct at time of going to press.

Author: Sarah Turner
Educational Consultant: Madeleine Barnes
Publisher: Laura White
Illustrator: Emily Skinner
Logo design: Amparo Barrera, Kneath Associates Ltd
Design: Julie Martin
Typesetting: Newgen
Cover design: Amparo Barrera, Kneath Associates Ltd
Project Manager: Sarah Bishop, Out of House Publishing
Copy Editor: Claire Pearce-Jones
Proofreader: Hayley Fairhead
Software development: Alex Morris

British Library Cataloguing–in–Publication Data
A CIP record for this book is available from the British Library.
Printed by Ashford Colour Press Ltd.

Contents

How to use this book

Most sections are presented as two pages, a teacher page for the teacher and a photocopiable pupil challenge page for the pupil. All answers are at the back of the book.

The layout is explained below.

1 Each teacher page begins with a 'Unit overview', outlining which objectives from the programme of study are covered.

2 The 'Subject knowledge' section has the main information about each topic, covering rules and principles. Where relevant, worked examples are shown.

3 Possible teaching steps suggest ways that the topic could be introduced to pupils, often building on previous knowledge. These need to be read before the lesson as some preparation may be necessary.

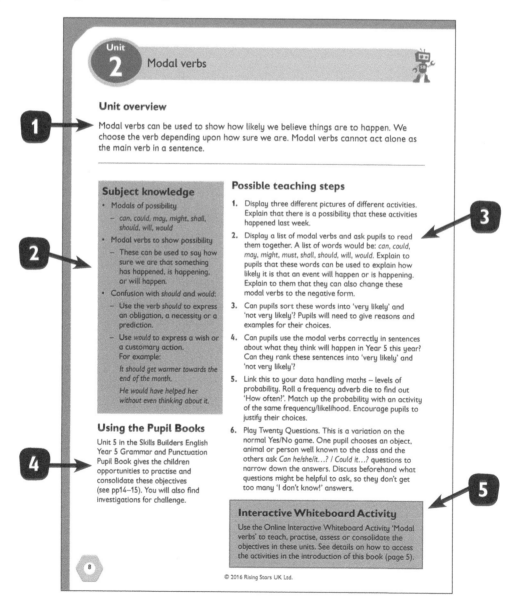

Unit 2 — Modal verbs

1 → **Unit overview**

Modal verbs can be used to show how likely we believe things are to happen. We choose the verb depending upon how sure we are. Modal verbs cannot act alone as the main verb in a sentence.

2 → **Subject knowledge**

- Modals of possibility
  - *can, could, may, might, shall, should, will, would*
- Modal verbs to show possibility
  - These can be used to say how sure we are that something has happened, is happening, or will happen.
- Confusion with *should* and *would*:
  - Use the verb *should* to express an obligation, a necessity or a prediction.
  - Use *would* to express a wish or a customary action.
    For example:
    It should get warmer towards the end of the month.
    He would have helped her without even thinking about it.

4 → **Using the Pupil Books**

Unit 5 in the Skills Builders English Year 5 Grammar and Punctuation Pupil Book gives the children opportunities to practise and consolidate these objectives (see pp14–15). You will also find investigations for challenge.

Possible teaching steps ← **3**

1. Display three different pictures of different activities. Explain that there is a possibility that these activities happened last week.
2. Display a list of modal verbs and ask pupils to read them together. A list of words would be: *can, could, may, might, must, shall, should, will, would.* Explain to pupils that these words can be used to explain how likely it is that an event will happen or is happening. Explain to them that they can also change these modal verbs to the negative form.
3. Can pupils sort these words into 'very likely' and 'not very likely'? Pupils will need to give reasons and examples for their choices.
4. Can pupils use the modal verbs correctly in sentences about what they think will happen in Year 5 this year? Can they rank these sentences into 'very likely' and 'not very likely'?
5. Link this to your data handling maths – levels of probability. Roll a frequency adverb die to find out 'How often?'. Match up the probability with an activity of the same frequency/likelihood. Encourage pupils to justify their choices.
6. Play Twenty Questions. This is a variation on the normal Yes/No game. One pupil chooses an object, animal or person well known to the class and the others ask *Can he/she/it…? / Could it…?* questions to narrow down the answers. Discuss beforehand what questions might be helpful to ask, so they don't get too many 'I don't know!' answers.

Interactive Whiteboard Activity ← **5**

Use the Online Interactive Whiteboard Activity 'Modal verbs' to teach, practise, assess or consolidate the objectives in these units. See details on how to access the activities in the introduction of this book (page 5).

8

4 Each unit clearly outlines the associated units and page references within the Skills Builders pupil books. This enables you to easily navigate between the books in the series.

5 Where there is a Skills Builders Interactive Whiteboard Activity alongside the unit, it is clearly outlined on the teacher page. Some online activities can be used to teach, practise, assess or consolidate knowledge across lots of units. To access the online interactive activities go to www.risingstars-uk.com and log into the My Rising Stars area. The Skills Builders interactive activities will be on your profile along with electronic versions of the Teacher Book.

6 The photocopiable pupil challenge can be used to practise, assess or consolidate knowledge. They might be used as homework activities. You can also find all answers on pages 58–63.

Modal verbs

Activity 1 Underline the modal verb in each of these sentences.

a) I think Eva could win the dancing medal tomorrow.

b) I will make you a birthday cake today.

c) We might have to cancel the trip if it continues to rain.

d) The window cleaner could fall off his ladder if he doesn't secure it properly.

e) The teacher will mark our tests today.

f) The painter could change his painting.

Activity 2 Re-write the sentences below, changing the modal verb.

a) They will come to the party tomorrow.

b) Maria may not be able to sing at the concert as she has lost her voice.

c) Jamie could win the race if he tries his best.

d) It will rain tomorrow just as the weather forecast says.

e) The school will open tomorrow for the children.

Activity 3 Tick the correct box to show whether these sentences show something is impossible, possible or certain.

6

	Impossible	Possible	Certain
The weather will be fine today.			
She must have been happy.			
Wisam couldn't have seen his brother playing.			
We could telephone the bus company.			
Adrian will be here by nine o'clock.			

9

Word class – nouns, verbs, conjunctions, pronouns, adverbs, prepositions and determiners

Unit overview

Words belong to different classes and each class has a different job to do within a sentence. Children in Year 5 need to have a secure understanding of a range of words including nouns, verbs, conjunctions, pronouns, adverbs, prepositions and determiners.

Subject knowledge

- Nouns tell you the name of a person, place, animal, thing or idea, for example, *girl, Matilda, Urmston, giraffe, imagination.*

- Verbs tell you what is happening in a sentence, for example, *hop.* They are often referred to as action words, but this is not always accurate, for example, the verb *to be.*

- Conjunctions make links between clauses, for example, *but, because, when, so, although.*

- Pronouns can stand in for a noun, for example, *I, she, he, we, they, my, his, her, their, it, mine, yours.*

- Adverbs fill in the detail about what is happening, for example, *suddenly, cheerfully, soon.*

- Prepositions tell you the position of things, for example, *up, over, after, through, by.*

- Determiners come before nouns or noun phrases and clarify the noun, for example, *a, the, this, that, those.*

Using the Pupil Books

Unit 1 in the Skills Builders English Year 5 Grammar and Punctuation Pupil Book gives the children opportunities to practise and consolidate these objectives (see pp4–7). You will also find investigations for challenge.

Possible teaching steps

1. Pupils will need to know what a sentence is. They will also need to know what each of the words mean and the functions they have.

2. Display sentences on the board. Can pupils identify the different word classes and the jobs they do?

3. Give pupils a piece of text you are using for your topic in humanities or science. Can they highlight the different types of words in the text?

4. Play Word Class Ping-Pong, in pairs or as a whole-class circle. The first child chooses a noun and the second child gives an adjective to go with it. The first pupil gives another noun to match the previous adjective. This could also be Verb/Adverb Ping-Pong.

5. Ask the pupils to make silly sentences by substituting a word for another word of the same class, for example *The huge elephant bounded through the trees.* Can they change *elephant* for another noun (e.g. apple)? Pupils could then change the verb and other word classes in the sentence.

6. Give pupils a list of nouns, for example, *computer, pen, chair, table, game, team, air* and *sheep.* Can they work out the correct determiner to go with each noun?

Interactive Whiteboard Activity

Use the Online Interactive Whiteboard Activity 'Word class' to teach, practise, assess or consolidate the objectives in these units. See details on how to access the activities in the introduction of this book (page 5).

Activity 1 — Circle the word class for each of the underlined words.

a) There was an <u>old</u> cabin next to the lake.

noun	verb	adjective

b) I had to <u>run</u> for the bus.

noun	verb	adjective

c) I'm going to <u>Spain</u> this summer.

noun	verb	adjective

d) He <u>crept</u> down the stairs quietly.

noun	verb	adjective

Activity 2 — Write *a* or *an* before each word.

a) _____ yacht

b) _____ hour

c) _____ obstacle

d) _____ drink

e) _____ example

f) _____ disappointment

g) _____ egg-timer

h) _____ aircraft

Activity 3 — Underline the determiners in these sentences.

a) A dog ran out into the road.

b) Rowan wanted an umbrella so he could make a costume for the party.

c) The card had a funny cartoon on the front.

d) Treat others the way you would like them to treat you.

Unit overview

Modal verbs can be used to show how likely we believe things are to happen. We choose the verb depending upon how sure we are. Modal verbs cannot act alone as the main verb in a sentence.

Subject knowledge

- Modals of possibility
  - *can, could, may, might, shall, should, will, would*
- Modal verbs to show possibility
  - These can be used to say how sure we are that something has happened, is happening, or will happen.
- Confusion with *should* and *would*:
  - Use the verb *should* to express an obligation, a necessity or a prediction.
  - Use *would* to express a wish or a customary action.
    For example:

    It should get warmer towards the end of the month.

    He would have helped her without even thinking about it.

Using the Pupil Books

Unit 5 in the Skills Builders English Year 5 Grammar and Punctuation Pupil Book gives the children opportunities to practise and consolidate these objectives (see pp14–15). You will also find investigations for challenge.

Possible teaching steps

1. Display three different pictures of different activities. Explain that there is a possibility that these activities happened last week.

2. Display a list of modal verbs and ask pupils to read them together. A list of words would be: *can, could, may, might, must, shall, should, will, would*. Explain to pupils that these words can be used to explain how likely it is that an event will happen or is happening. Explain to them that they can also change these modal verbs to the negative form.

3. Can pupils sort these words into 'very likely' and 'not very likely'? Pupils will need to give reasons and examples for their choices.

4. Can pupils use the modal verbs correctly in sentences about what they think will happen in Year 5 this year? Can they rank these sentences into 'very likely' and 'not very likely'?

5. Link this to your data handling maths – levels of probability. Roll a frequency adverb die to find out 'How often?'. Match up the probability with an activity of the same frequency/likelihood. Encourage pupils to justify their choices.

6. Play Twenty Questions. This is a variation on the normal Yes/No game. One pupil chooses an object, animal or person well known to the class and the others ask *Can he/she/it…? / Could it…?* questions to narrow down the answers. Discuss beforehand what questions might be helpful to ask, so they don't get too many 'I don't know!' answers.

Interactive Whiteboard Activity

Use the Online Interactive Whiteboard Activity 'Modal verbs' to teach, practise, assess or consolidate the objectives in these units. See details on how to access the activities in the introduction of this book (page 5).

Activity 1 — Underline the modal verb in each of these sentences.

a) I think Eva could win the dancing medal tomorrow.

b) I will make you a birthday cake today.

c) We might have to cancel the trip if it continues to rain.

d) The window cleaner could fall off his ladder if he doesn't secure it properly.

e) The teacher will mark our tests today.

f) The painter could change his painting.

Activity 2 — Re-write the sentences below, changing the modal verb.

a) They will come to the party tomorrow.

b) Maria may not be able to sing at the concert as she has lost her voice.

c) Jamie could win the race if he tries his best.

d) It will rain tomorrow just as the weather forecast says.

e) The school will open tomorrow for the children.

Activity 3 — Tick the correct box to show whether these sentences show something is impossible, possible or certain.

	Impossible	Possible	Certain
The weather will be fine today.			
She must have been happy.			
Wisam couldn't have seen his brother playing.			
We could telephone the bus company.			
Adrian will be here by nine o'clock.			

Unit overview

Clauses contain a subject doing a verb. Main (independent) clauses can stand alone as simple sentences or be part of other sentences. Clauses can be combined to make compound and complex sentences.

Phrases do not have a subject doing a verb. They are a group of words that function as a single word. A phrase is one of the basic building blocks of a sentence.

Subject knowledge

- **Main (or independent) clauses**
  - Main clauses have a subject and a verb and form a complete thought, for example:

    The cat purred. (clause)/*The cat purred.* (simple sentence)

  - If a sentence doesn't have a main clause, it is actually a fragment, for example, *The dog wearing the collar.* Here, *dog* is the subject and *wearing the collar* is an adjectival phrase that helps the reader identify the dog.

- Combining clauses
  - Two main clauses can be put together to form a compound or complex sentence. They must be joined by a conjunction, for example:

    The dog barked and the cat ran up a tree.

- **Phrases**
  - A phrase is a group of words that are linked together in meaning and act as a single word in a sentence.

Possible teaching steps

1. Display a range of clauses and phrases. Can pupils sort them into phrases and clauses, and explain their reasons why? Ask them to mark/highlight all the verbs.

2. Discuss the results. Explain that the difference between a phrase and a clause is that a group of words without a verb is a phrase.

3. Next, ask pupils to work with a partner to highlight the subjects (nouns and pronouns that are doing the verb). Groups of words without a subject doing the verb are a phrase. Can they create three phrases and three clauses using the rules?

4. Add in a clause – when modelling or sharing writing on the board, ask the pupils *Why?* and *When?* to elicit extra information, then demonstrate how to edit the new clause into the original sentence.

5. Direct pupils to your 'Tell me more!' display and encourage them to add new clauses to a sentence of the day from your class novel or other text.

6. Deliberately leave an opening subordinate clause unconnected to a main clause in your modelled writing. Firstly, does the class recognise your 'error', and secondly, can they suggest a fitting main clause to complete the sentence?

Using the Pupil Books

Unit 2 in the Skills Builders English Year 5 Grammar and Punctuation Pupil Book gives the children opportunities to practise and consolidate these objectives (see pp8–10). You will also find investigations for challenge.

Activity 1

Can you complete the sentences by writing a subordinate clause to follow the independent clause?

Independent clause	Subordinate clause
We will go to the fair	
Put on your coat	
I'd love a slice of cake	
You should sit down	
Put a tick next to it	
It should be fine	

Activity 2

Underline the main clause in each of these sentences.

a) As soon as the meat was eaten, the lions strolled away.

b) I sent a letter that arrived a week late.

c) My sister, who lives with me, loves dogs.

d) Do you know the boy who is wearing the football shirts?

e) I ate the fruit that was in the fruit bowl.

f) I really enjoyed the new film that we watched last night.

Activity 3

Choose a word from the box to join these clauses and make compound sentences.

and	so	for	yet	nor	but	or

a) Running was hard _____ I preferred to walk.

b) The food was delicious _____ I couldn't eat it.

c) Would he work _____ would he just sit there?

d) Javid was tired _____ he still carried on.

Unit 4 — Expanded noun phrases

Unit overview

An expanded noun phrase includes a noun and an adjective to describe it. It gives more information about the noun.

Subject knowledge

- In an expanded noun phrase, words are added to the noun to provide more information.
- A noun phrase is made up of a noun and any words that are modifying that noun, including articles, determiners and adjectives or adjectival phrases. Noun phrases work in exactly the same way as nouns in a sentence.

Using the Pupil Books

Unit 6 in the Skills Builders English Year 5 Grammar and Punctuation Pupil Books gives the children opportunities to practise and consolidate these objectives (see pp16–17). You will also find investigations for challenge.

Possible teaching steps

1. Give the children an object. Can the children add adjectives before the noun to describe it? Ask the children to find the longest sentences to describe the object. Repeat this with other objects around the room.

2. Ask the children to read a page from their favourite book or current reading book. Can they highlight as many noun phrases as possible? Children could have a competition to find the longest list of noun phrases in the class.

3. Share with the children the sentence: *The cat chased the mouse.* How can we make this more interesting by adding as many noun phrases as possible? Write down as many different possibilities that the children come up with. Can they use a thesaurus to extend the adjectives used?

4. Pupils could add expanded noun phrases to add interest and variety to their own writing.

5. Display the sentence: *The boy lifted his eyes to the sky.* Ask the pupils to identify the nouns. Then display the sentence: *The frightened four-year-old boy from Devon lifted his tear-filled, bruised eyes to the threatening, snow-filled night sky.* Ask the pupils to identify the noun phrases. Discuss the impact of the noun phrases.

Interactive Whiteboard Activity

Use the Online Interactive Whiteboard Activity 'Expanded noun phrases' to teach, practise, assess or consolidate the objectives in these units. See details on how to access the activities in the introduction of this book (page 5).

Activity 1
Underline all the expanded noun phrases in the following paragraph.

The fast and skilful footballer scored the first magnificent goal. It turned out that this amazing goal was the only one of the damp and boring game of football. The angry crowd shouted and booed loudly at their usually fantastic team. After the match the long-standing manager was sacked and they replaced him with a new and improved one. The fanatical fans hope that this new manager will win the all important trophy at the end of the season.

Activity 2
Can you add extra information before and after the noun?

Article		Noun		
The		buns		tasted nice.
The		man		looked at the picture.
He had a		car		
The		yacht		sailed away.

Activity 3
Tick the sentences that contain a noun phrase.

Let's go to the park.

Have you seen my new bicycle seat?

Please pass me the packet of crisps.

Sarah can run very quickly.

Activity 4
Which of the sentences below contain noun phrases?

Large bikes are not allowed on the playground.

Please stop at the road.

Jo took her sister's new sparkly dress.

You are smaller yet stronger than me.

Unit overview

Pronouns are used to replace nouns or noun phrases. Using pronouns avoids repetition in writing.

Subject knowledge

- Relative pronouns link one part of a sentence to another by introducing a relative clause that describes an earlier noun or pronoun.

- Examples are *who, whom, whose, which, that, what.*

    For example, *The way **that** is shorter is best.*

Using the Pupil Books

Unit 7 in the Skills Builders English Year 5 Grammar and Punctuation Pupil Book gives the children opportunities to practise and consolidate these objectives (see pp18–19). You will also find investigations for challenge.

Possible teaching steps

1. Write a simple sentence in big letters on the laminated poster and place slips of paper/post-its nearby. Pupils write an extended version of the sentence with a relative pronoun clause and stick it to the poster.

2. In modelling any kind of paragraph writing, stop after a simple sentence. Ask pupils to help you edit and improve by adding extra information with a relative pronoun, either as a drop-in clause or with the subordinate clause at the end (whichever is your focus).

3. Deliberately leave in the noun/pronoun which the relative pronoun has replaced in your shared text. Can they spot the error?

4. To reinforce how a complex sentence is constructed, highlight a complex sentence which uses a relative clause and break it back down into two shorter sentences. Can they 'fill in the gaps' if the simple sentences don't quite make sense?

5. Deliberately use an object relative clause in modelled writing (e.g. *She recognised the man who/that she'd seen earlier*), get them to identify the relative pronoun, and then muse aloud about whether it could be left out. Ask pupils if the sentence means the same thing with/without. Which sounds more effective?

6. Show the children the following passage. Can they choose *who, which* or *whose* to complete the text?

    Tim Peake is a famous astronaut _____ was born on the 7th April 1972. The mission in _____ he has recently been involved has been widely covered by the media. Tim, _____ spent six years training for the mission of a lifetime, has two children _____ names are Oliver and Thomas. They went to watch their father's rocket launch, _____ took place in Kazakhstan.

Activity 1 — Can you circle the relative pronoun in each of the sentences?

a) My teacher, who is called Miss Kinlock, comes from America.

b) Shelly, who is always late for work, needs to set her alarm.

c) The Mediterranean, where many people travel to, is only a couple of hours from England.

d) There isn't any more pizza, which is my favourite thing to eat.

e) The sisters, who like princesses, went to watch Cinderella at the cinema.

f) The restaurant, which is the best in the city, was overbooked on Saturday.

Activity 2 — Rearrange each pair of sentences so the relative pronoun (in brackets) and extra information clause are in the middle.

a) Chocolate contains 'feel good' chemicals. Chocolate originates in South America. (which)

b) The Queen is one of the richest women in the world. She owns several castles. (who)

c) At eight o'clock last night I went to bed. I had finished my homework then. (when)

d) Phillip Pullman is my favourite writer. He wrote *Clockwork*. (who)

e) Ostriches are the world's largest birds. Ostriches live in Africa. (that)

f) We are having fishcakes for tea. I hate fishcakes. (which)

Activity 3 — Choose from the words *who, whose* or *which* to complete these sentences.

a) The cat, _____ liked milk, is called Fluffy.

b) This is the packet _____ I opened for my sister.

c) This is the girl _____ name is Frances.

d) The cake _____ I baked for my friend, was a great success.

Unit overview

Paragraphs are used to indicate shifts in time, place or character in fiction. In non-fiction they are used for different themes, subjects or topics.

Subject knowledge

- A new paragraph is used to signal something new. In narrative, this may be used to indicate a shift in time, place or character. For time and place, conjunctions can be used to show cohesion, for example, *Later that day…, The next morning…, Eventually…, At the market…, Further along the road…, As they arrived at Robert's house….*

- In non-fiction, the topic or paragraph is described in one sentence, called a topic sentence. The sentences that follow then give more detail. This can be remembered as:

  P = point (topic sentence)

  E = evidence

  E = explanation.

- Conjunctions can also be used to link paragraphs in non-fiction, for example *First…, However…, As a result…, In addition to…, Finally….*

Using the Pupil Books

Units 8 and 9 in the Skills Builders English Year 5 Grammar and Punctuation Pupil Book give the children opportunities to practise and consolidate these objectives (see pp20–23). You will also find investigations for challenge.

Possible teaching steps

1. Pupils will need to organise more extended narratives into several basic paragraphs that relate to story structure. In non-fiction texts they will need to organise the texts into paragraphs that separate the different aspects of the topic. They will need to set out the paragraphs using lines between each one and use conjunctions for cohesion.

2. Give pupils a piece of text that has been chopped up into paragraphs and ask them to put them back together so that it makes sense.

3. Share with pupils a story opener and a basic plot. Can they write three more paragraphs to continue the story? Can they use paragraphs correctly? Do pupils use conjunctions to show a shift in time or place?

4. Can pupils create a list of conjunctions that are used to link paragraphs in fiction and non-fiction?

5. Using narrative as an example: use events from the class reader and stick these words around the room (*before, after that, first* and *finally*). Write an event from the story on the board and then suggest other events – pupils move to the correct word depending on whether the event happened before or after.

6. Non-fiction – using a science topic, list a number of facts about the topic. Can pupils then create paragraphs about this subject? Ensure there is a clear topic sentence to start, and then give evidence to support the topic sentence and finally an explanation (using PEE to structure each paragraph). Remind pupils of the conjunctions used for cohesion in non-fiction texts.

Activity 1   Can you rearrange the story below so that it is in the correct order? Use the topic sentence and events to help you put the paragraphs in the right order.

A bump in the night

a)	Then all of a sudden there was a shadow forming on the old and decaying wall. Sarah shuddered and stood still with fear. The hairs on the back of her neck stood up and the silence was deafening.
b)	Sarah walked, in the dark, along the path and up to the old, wooden door. It looked like nobody had lived there for years. There were cobwebs and tattered old curtains, which had seen better days, hanging in the dusty windows.
c)	A bump and the slam of a door could be heard from the next room. Sarah could feel warm air flowing through her hair. She dared not turn round. It was bound to be something sinister. She ran for her life out of the old abandoned house.
d)	She opened the door, using the metal door handle and looked around the vast hallway. It used to be a magnificent building but had been left to fall apart by the previous owner. Carefully she walked up the stairs to explore the bedrooms.

Activity 2   Looking at the paragraphs above, can you identify and write out the topic sentence from each one?

a) _____

b) _____

c) _____

d) _____

Activity 3   Can you finish off this paragraph? The topic sentence has been written for you.

The forest fire raged. _____

_____

_____

_____

Revision – Adverbials and fronted adverbials

Unit overview

An adverbial is a word or phrase that gives more information about a verb. Adverbs, prepositional phrases and subordinating phrases can all be used as adverbials. A fronted adverbial is a word or phrase that comes at the beginning of a sentence, and is used to describe the action that follows.

Subject knowledge

- **Adverbials**
  - Adverbials answer questions such as *When? Where? Why? How often?* and *How?*
  - Adverbials are usually, but not always, written at the end of a sentence, for example:

    We went walking over the local hills on Sunday.

- **Fronted adverbials**
  - This is the term used for adverbials that are used at the start of a sentence. They are usually followed by a comma, for example:

    On Sunday, we went walking over the hills.

- **Conjunctions in adverbials**
  - Adverbials often start with conjunctions, for example, *because, as, when, after, as soon as, in order to, so that, although, if, in case.*

Using the Pupil Books

Unit 10 in the Skills Builders English Year 5 Grammar and Punctuation Pupil Book gives the children opportunities to practise and consolidate these objectives (see pp24–25). You will also find investigations for challenge.

Possible teaching steps

1. Give the pupils a simple sentence, for example, *Kirsty went for a walk.* Ask the pupils to talk to a partner and think of all the questions they could ask about this sentence and the character Kirsty. A pupil could pretend to be Kirsty and hot seat questions they might ask her. Pupils will need to ask: *Where? When? Why? How often? How far? Who with? How fast?* Collect and discuss the questions and possible responses.

2. Ask the pupils to work with a shoulder partner and add information to the first sentence to answer one of the questions that was asked of Kirsty. An example of this could be, *Kirsty went for a walk to the shops to buy a pint of milk.*

3. Collect and discuss the sentences pupils have created. Explain that the information they have added to the sentences are called adverbials.

4. Fronted adverbials will also need to be taught to add variety to sentences. Pupils will need to know that a comma follows a fronted adverbial. Share with them the sentence: *Next week, I am flying to Jamaica.* The first part of the sentence answers the question *When?* Explain to pupils that we can change a sentence around to write the adverbial at the front/beginning of a sentence. They can use some of their sentences from earlier tasks to change the adverbial to a fronted adverbial.

5. Pupils will need to be taught that commas follow a fronted adverbial. Give the pupils an example of an event, for example, *I went to Russia.* Ask the pupils to suggest an adverb of time (*When I went to Russia*). Scribe their ideas on to a flip chart or whiteboard. Demonstrate how some of their suggestions can be moved before the verb and read together. Repeat, trying other adverbials, and discuss why and how some work and others don't. Challenge the pupils to use fronted adverbial of time (*When?*), place (*Where?*) and manner (*How?/Why?*).

Activity 1   Use adverbs to modify these clauses.

a) Ben ran _____.

b) She yawned _____.

c) I ate my breakfast _____.

d) The ball fell _____.

e) The room went _____ dark.

Activity 2   Use adverbial phrases to modify these clauses.

a) Azan whacked the ball _____.

b) The builders built the house _____.

c) It rained _____.

d) I'm going to a party _____.

Activity 3   Use fronted adverbials to modify these clauses.

a) _____ I'm playing tennis.

b) _____ I tidied my room.

c) _____ the lightning struck the tree.

d) _____ we are going to the seaside.

e) _____ I tried again.

f) _____ Dad was cleaning the kitchen.

Present perfect form and past perfect tense

Unit overview

Perfect forms of verbs are used to mark the relationship of time and clause.

Subject knowledge

- Perfect forms of verbs mark relationships of time and clause, for example, *I have finished my chores so we can go to the park.*

- Present perfect form
  - Present perfect forms of verbs are used when we want to write about something that has happened in the past, but we do not specify the time.

  - Common irregular verbs: *think/ thought, eat/ate, blow/blew, take/ took, wear/wore, drive/drove, creep/crept, ring/rang, make/made, buy/bought, is/was, send/sent, bite/ bit, shake/shook, are/were, drink/ drank, know/knew, sit/sat, meet/ met, write/wrote.*

- Past perfect tense

- The past perfect tense describes an action that happened in the past before something else happened. It is formed in the same way as the present perfect tense, but uses the auxiliary verb form *had* before the past participle, for example, *I had escaped.*

Using the Pupil Books

Units 11 and 12 Grammar and Punctuation Pupil Book give the children opportunities to practise and consolidate these objectives (see pp26–29). You will also find investigations for challenge.

Possible teaching steps

1. Ask pupils to identify verbs in the following text: *My Grandad has played the trumpet for ten years and has been playing in concerts all that time. Before he played the trumpet, he used to play football but he got bored of this so he changed to the trumpet!.* Then divide into finished (past) or unfinished (present/present perfect) actions.

2. Pupils choose the correct tense between present perfect or past simple in the following sentences:

   *I **went** to the park yesterday./I **have been** to the park yesterday.*

   *When you **have finished** your homework, you can go and play./When you **finished** your homework, you can go and play.*

   *I **have lost** my favourite jumper during the last lesson./ I **lost** my favourite jumper during last lesson.*

3. Explain to pupils that the present perfect tense uses the auxiliary verb **have** before the main verb.

   Use **have** for I/you/we/they.

   Use **has** for he/she/it.

   a) I **have been** to the park yesterday.

   b) When you **have finished** your homework, you can go and play.

   c) I **have lost** my jumper during the last lesson.

   Highlight the verb 'to have' in examples a–d above. Explain to pupils that this is absent when writing the past simple form. Hold up examples of sentences where the present perfect tense is used and the past simple tense. Pupils can put thumbs up or down to say if the sentences are written correctly.

4. Group matching activity – pupils match infinitive (main form) of verb with the correct past participle to support further work on using the present perfect tense. Words to use: *do, done, be, been, have, had, get, got, come, come, go, gone, begin, begun, grow, grown, forget, forgotten, read, read, bite, bitten, choose, chosen.*

Activity 1

Put the verb(s) in brackets into simple past tense to complete the sentence.

a) When you (watch) the play, did you notice the mouse on the stage?

b) I (have) a packet of crisps, so I (eat) them.

c) Jennie (knock) on the door earlier to drop off a present.

d) Justin (cry) when he (fall) over.

Activity 2

Underline the sentences that are written in the present tense.

a) The children were learning about the Tudors.

b) She was carefully pouring milk from the bottle.

c) The computer isn't working now!

d) The teachers chose the trip for the children to go on.

e) Alex is learning to ride her bike.

Activity 3

Write either the word *present* or *past* at the end of each sentence to show which tense it has been written in. Underline the verbs to show the tense choice.

a) The lions roar loudly in the jungle.

b) Danielle had her own pony for nine years.

c) It has been a great week as it was my birthday.

d) Tom ate his lunch with his friends.

e) The ice is melting in the summer sun.

f) The baby is walking for the first time.

Unit overview

A singular subject takes a singular verb. A plural subject takes a plural verb.

Subject knowledge

- If two subjects are linked in a sentence, follow these rules when deciding whether to use a singular or plural verb.

First subject	Connecting word	Second subject	Verb
singular	and	singular	plural
singular	or	singular	singular
singular	or	plural	plural

- Pronouns such as *anybody*, *anyone*, *each*, *everyone*, *somebody* and *someone* are singular and should have singular verbs.

  Amounts of money and time use a singular verb.

- Collective nouns can be singular depending on the context in the sentence. An example of this would be:

  *The team **is** well prepared. All of the team **are** well prepared.*

Using the Pupil Books

Unit 13 in the Skills Builders English Year 5 Grammar and Punctuation Pupil Book gives the children opportunities to practise and consolidate these objectives (see pp30–31). You will also find investigations for challenge.

Possible teaching steps

1. To decide if a verb is singular or plural, use *he* and *they*: *he thinks* (so *thinks* is singular); *they think* (so *think* is plural). Ask pupils to think of other examples to record.

2. Ask different groups of pupils to conjugate the verb *to be* in different tenses. Record these on a board or large sheet of paper. For example:

   present: *I am, you are, he/she is, we are, you are, they are*

   past: *I was, you were, he/she was, we were, you were, they were*

   but **future**: *I will be, you will be, he/she will be, we will be, you will be, they will be.*

   Look for misconceptions and correct where necessary.

3. Give pupils sentences with the verb *to be* missing. Ask them to work together to fill in the missing verb. Example sentences could be: *The girls _____ singing now. The cows _____ out yesterday.*

4. Explain that you have cut 'was' or 'were' out of each sentence. Ask pupils to work with a partner, putting the correct word back into each sentence. Collect and display the responses, correcting them as necessary. Establish that 'was' and 'were' are the past tense of the verb *to be*. Demonstrate how to conjugate the past tense of the verb *to be* and then ask pupils to conjugate it with a partner.

Activity 1 — Circle the verbs that need changing in these sentences.

a) We was going to the cinema.

b) The children always slides on the grass.

c) Maisie and Leo was pleased to get a day off school.

d) If Joel or Callum are early, ask them to help you.

e) Ayaan and the girls rides last Monday night.

Activity 2 — Write *talk* or *talks* to complete each sentence correctly.

a) If Wisam or Cody _____, send them to the head teacher.

b) When Liam and Ethan _____ they don't know when to stop!

c) The teachers and the parents _____ about us too often.

d) Lauren and the children _____ really loudly in the canteen.

e) Vicky or the children _____ to Mr Walsh every morning.

Activity 3 — Cross out the incorrect verb forms and write them correctly. Use the present tense.

a) I wonder why you always shouts at me. _____

b) She go to her acting class every week. _____

c) I heard Jake and Layla falls off the wall. _____

d) Didn't you know that Max and Rio is in the shed? _____

e) The ball and the posts is on the field. _____

Unit overview

'I' and 'me' are both personal pronouns. In Standard English, it is important to use 'I' and 'me' correctly.

Subject knowledge

- **Personal pronouns 'I' and 'me'**

  In sentences where they stand alone, it is usually straightforward to know whether to use 'I' or 'me', for example:

  I carried the heaviest suitcase.

  Mr Dale asked me to adjust the settings on the computer.

- When the pronouns 'I' and 'me' are used in conjunction with people, mistakes can be made.

- Checking for correct use of 'I' and 'me':

  – Consider the sentences:

    The party was hosted by Tom and I.

    The party was hosted by Tom and me.

  – Try out the sentences using only the first person pronoun. This gives:

    The party was hosted by I.

    The party was hosted by me.

  – It is now evident that the correct pronoun is 'me' and the full sentence is:

    The party was hosted by Tom and me.

  – The same rule applies when the conjunction *or* is used:

    You could ask Gill or me.

    Either Gill or I could do it.

Possible teaching steps

1. Give pupils a range of sentences where 'I' or 'me' are missing. Ask them to fill in the correct word. Example sentences could be:

   Jakub and _____ sent the email to the club.

   The trip was planned by Clarissa and _____.

2. Share with pupils the rules about adding 'I' or 'me' and the tips for doing this. (See 'Subject knowledge' for details of this.)

3. Ask the pupils to think of other sentences where they will need to choose the word 'I' or 'me'. They could create sentences for others to try.

4. Share with the children the following sentences:

   I wanted Dad to watch _____ in the football match.

   He walked to school with Danny and _____.

   My teacher told Terry and _____ to collect the books.

   Eddie came to school with Jim and _____.

   Ben and _____ are going to the cinema tomorrow.

   Discuss with the children whether to add 'I' or 'me' and their reasons for this. If the children are still finding it difficult to choose the correct word, go through the rules again.

Interactive Whiteboard Activity

Use the Online Interactive Whiteboard Activity 'I and me' to teach, practise, assess or consolidate the objectives in these units. See details on how to access the activities in the introduction of this book (page 5).

Activity 1 — Choose 'I' or 'me' to complete the following sentences.

a) Can you help (I/me) to finish the lunch?

b) When the rain stops, Megan and (I/me) are going for a walk.

c) Amisha is a great dancer, I'm sure she would dance for you and (I/me).

d) Would you go to the shops for (I/me), so that I can watch the end of the film?

e) It was a late night for Tia and (I/me) as we went to watch the football.

f) Next year Leo and (I/me) are getting married.

Activity 2 — Tick the sentences where 'I' or 'me' has been used correctly.

a) Next week, my dad and I are going to the cinema to see the latest film. ☐

b) You should not be copying Simon and I, we might not have the correct answers. ☐

c) Me and my sister will come to the party if our mum can drop us off. ☐

d) George and me went to watch the rugby match at the weekend. ☐

e) The painter and I were creating a masterpiece. ☐

Activity 3 — Complete the text correctly by writing 'I' or 'me'.

If you and _____ were travelling to Manchester, _____ would travel on a train. It would be easier for Sandra and _____ to drive as _____ have lots of luggage to take with _____. When we get there, Sandra and _____ will visit the main attractions. _____ especially like the old buildings. Sandra and _____ are going to have a wonderful trip!

Unit 11
Changing nouns or adjectives into verbs using suffixes -ate, -ise, -ify and -en

Unit overview

Suffixes are groups of letters attached to the end of a root word. Suffixes can change the word class.

Subject knowledge

- Converting nouns to verbs

These examples show how nouns and adjectives can be converted to verbs using the suffixes -ate, -ise, -ify and -en.

- Adding -ate to nouns and adjectives:

  alien/alienate, captive/captivate, active/activate

- Adding -ise to nouns and adjectives:

  liquid/liquidise, magnet/ magnetise, real/realise

- Adding -ify to nouns and adjectives:

  beauty/beautify, person/ personify, test/testify

- Adding -en to nouns and adjectives:

  threat/threaten, fright/frighten, broad/broaden

Using the Pupil Books

Unit 15 in the Skills Builders English Year 5 Grammar and Punctuation Pupil Book gives the children opportunities to practise and consolidate these objectives (see pp34–35). You will also find investigations for challenge.

Possible teaching steps

1. Display a set of words from the same word family that have different word classes, for example, *magnet*.

2. Ask the pupils to work with a partner and decide the word class of each word created. Pupils should work with a partner and use each word in a sentence to demonstrate the word class. Collect and discuss the sentences created. Agree that *magnet* is a noun, the word *magnetic* is an adjective, *magnetise* and *magnify* are both verbs.

3. Ask pupils to identify the suffixes on the verbs (-ify and -ise).

4. Give pupils other word families such as *liquid*, *sense* and *apology*. Can they create adjectives and verbs using the suffixes?

5. Can pupils come up with other words where you can create a noun, adjective and verb by using the suffixes above?

6. Pupils learn the rules and practise applying them by sorting word cards or sticky notes in groups. Each group can create their own grid on a large piece of paper. Ask pupils to try putting together different roots and different endings. Ask the children to think about whether the word sounds silly or if it is a real word.

Activity 1

Change these nouns to verbs and use the verb in a sentence.

Noun	Verb	Sentence
pollen		
note		
drama		
author		
light		

Activity 2

Change these adjectives to verbs and use the verb in a sentence.

Adjective	Verb	Sentence
solid		
simple		
legal		
sweet		
active		

Activity 3

Change the underlined noun in each sentence to a verb by adding a suffix.

a) Blanka warned us that birds terror her.

b) The band needs to advert for a new member.

c) The odd looking creature was hard to class.

Activity 4

Complete each sentence by choosing the verb with the correct suffix.

a) The head-teacher had to _____ parents that school would be closed due to the snow. (noten/notify)

b) As the sun came out, the day began to _____ (brightise/brighten).

c) The teacher had to _____ the ball. (confiscify/confiscate)

27

Unit overview

Verb prefixes modify the meaning of the verb but do not change the word class.

Subject knowledge

- Prefix meanings

  dis- gives the opposite meaning

  mis- wrongly or badly

  de- do the opposite

  over- too much

  re- again or back

  co- together with

  out- more or better than others

  pre- before or in front of

- Understanding the use of prefixes

  - To check that a word has a prefix it is necessary to identify the root word. If there is no root word, then the letter string at the start is not a prefix, for example, *disturb*: 'turb' is not a verb so the 'dis' at the start of the word is not a prefix.

  - If there is a root word, then the prefix adds to the meaning of the word, for example, *use* (to employ), *misuse* (to use wrongly).

- Using hyphens with prefixes

  - If a prefix ends with a vowel and the root word starts with a vowel, hyphens can be used to avoid confusion, for example, *re-employ*.

  - If a root word with a prefix could be confused with another word, then a hyphen is used to distinguish the words, for example, *recover* (from an illness), *re-cover* (a chair seat).

Possible teaching steps

1. Display the verb *to change*. Ask pupils to use a dictionary to find all the meanings of *to change* that are verbs. Ask them to discuss with a partner all the ways of changing the meaning while still using the verb *to change*. Share and record pupils' ideas. Focus on the use of prefixes in changing the verb meaning.

2. Challenge pupils to work with a partner and find different prefixes that can be used with the verb *to change* and the meanings that are conveyed.

3. Each pair will have a set of prefix cards and a sheet of root words. They are to match up the root words and prefixes to make proper words; they are then to write the words that they find in their books. Pupils are to work on one prefix at a time.

4. Pupils may make up their own words; they will be encouraged to check any words they are unsure of in a dictionary.

5. Give the pupils a set of root words (on white cards) and a set of prefixes (on blue cards). Test each root word with each prefix and identify any new words that are created. Ask pupils to work with a partner to recreate the words and write them down.

Using the Pupil Books

Unit 16 in the Skills Builders English Year 5 Grammar and Punctuation Pupil Book gives the children opportunities to practise and consolidate these objectives (see pp36–37). You will also find investigations for challenge.

Activity 1

Prefixes go at the beginning of words. This changes the meaning of the word.

Can you complete the table below all about prefixes?

Prefix	Meaning	Example word	Other words
dis			
de			
mis			
over			
re			
pre			

Activity 2

Can you draw a line to match the prefix, meaning and root words in the table below?

Prefix	Root word	Meaning
de	throne	fill too much
over	rail	remove from a throne
dis	build	show lack of respect
re	respect	build again
mis	fill	cause a train to leave the track
de	take	get something wrong

Activity 3

Add prefixes to give these verbs the opposite meaning.

a) _____ appear

b) _____ behave

c) _____ use

d) _____ tie

e) _____ continue

f) _____ run

Unit overview

A parenthesis is a word or phrase added as an explanation, to provide extra information, as an afterthought or as an aside in a sentence that would be complete without it. Parentheses are usually punctuated with commas, brackets or dashes. Brackets themselves are also called parentheses.

Subject knowledge

- Examples of parentheses
  - As an explanation: *Photosynthesis (the process of converting sunlight to food) is used by most plants.*
  - As an aside: *She was lying (what a surprise) and no one seemed to realise.*
  - To add additional information: *New employees (especially students) find it difficult to adjust to the workplace.*
  - To add an example as a list: *My friends – Ann, Aiden and Oliver – are in Florida this week.*
- Punctuating parentheses
  - Punctuating with brackets is the most common way to punctuate a parenthesis.
  - Punctuating with commas gives parenthesis less emphasis than brackets.
  - Punctuating with dashes gives the parenthesis more emphasis than brackets.

Using the Pupil Books

Unit 17 in the Skills Builders English Year 5 Grammar and Punctuation Pupil Book gives the children opportunities to practise and consolidate these objectives (see pp38–39). You will also find investigations for challenge.

Possible teaching steps

1. Display this sentence: *The students were very noisy.* Ask pupils for any additional information they could give about the students. If necessary, prompt them with questions. Discuss and record their ideas.

2. Select a suitable addition and demonstrate how to add this information and punctuate it correctly: *The students (being excited) were very noisy.*

3. Look for parenthesis markers in shared texts, either as a whole class or with a guided reading group. Make sure your pupils can identify which noun/noun phrases or clause is being extended by the parenthetical phrases.

4. Relate parenthesis to work you may have done already on relative clauses.

5. In groups, build a human sentence, then add parenthesis to each noun/noun phrase, using the correct punctuation. How long can you make the sentence?

6. As a morning work task, write a simple sentence on the board and challenge the class to add parenthesis to it.

Interactive Whiteboard Activity

Use the Online Interactive Whiteboard Activity 'Brackets' to teach, practise, assess or consolidate the objectives in these units. See details on how to access the activities in the introduction of this book (page 5).

Activity 1

Put brackets around the parenthesis in these sentences.

a) David talks all the time he never stops and it drives us all mad.

b) My dog has had a litter of puppies three in total and they are all white.

c) My favourite book is Cinderella I only like traditional tales.

d) Megan who has been practising her somersaults will be entering the competition today.

e) Goats although renowned for eating almost anything mostly eat grass, bushes and leaves.

f) The teacher who enjoyed singing started a choir at her school.

Activity 2

For each of these sentences, add an extra information clause to the noun clause in bold.

Remember to mark the start and end of your parenthesis with brackets, commas or dashes.

a) I'm going to **a party** on Saturday.

b) At the zoo last week, we saw **five elephants**.

c) Never smile at **a crocodile** or you'll regret it!

d) Mum's promised us **hot chocolate** after swimming club.

Activity 3

Rewrite each of these sentences and choose a suitable parenthesis from the boxes to add more information.

a Ford Fiesta	he's called Eric	who is called Mr Taylor
the kind with the flip screen	20 metres high	which is next to the basketball

a) The car was left by the side of the road.

b) My favourite teacher let us have ice-cream today.

c) The football is the best choice.

d) My friend is coming round for dinner.

e) My new phone is amazing!

f) The Angel of the North is near Gateshead.

Unit 14 Commas to clarify meaning and avoid ambiguity

Unit overview

Commas are used to help clarify meaning in a sentence. They can help avoid ambiguity.

Subject knowledge

- When to use commas

  These are the most important uses of commas for pupils to learn:

  - In lists, to separate words and word groups in a list or more than two items.

  - Between adjectives, when the word and could be inserted between them, for example, a long, hard road (which has a comma as you could say a long and hard road).

  - After subordinate clauses, put a comma before the main clause, for example, *Although she was new, she seemed very confident.*

  - Before inverted commas, if they are used mid-sentence and have no other punctuation before them, for example, *Daria said, 'I have finished.'*

  - Before a question tag, for example, *'You didn't go, did you?'*

Using the Pupil Books

Unit 18 in the Skills Builders English Year 5 Grammar and Punctuation Pupil Book gives the children opportunities to practise and consolidate these objectives (see pp40–41). You will also find investigations for challenge.

Possible teaching steps

1. Display a sentence, for example, *The bus was late.* Display a set of words and phrases that could be used in the sentence, for example, *however, nevertheless, well, which was full, which got a puncture, actually.* Demonstrate how to cut the sentence and put in an extra word or phrase into the sentence. Demonstrate how commas show the cut point in the sentence or at the start, for example, *The bus, however, was late./ However, the bus was late.* Ask pupils to create their own sentences using commas.

2. As a morning task or lesson opener activity, write a simple sentence (e.g. *I went to the zoo.*) on your whiteboard. Challenge pupils to come up with at least three adverbial opening phrases. They then read the new sentence aloud to their partner/the class, using physical punctuation.

3. Play 'pass the sentence' on mini whiteboards. Give pupils a starting word for their opening adverbial phrase, which they write on their whiteboard. Each pupil passes their board to the next person round the group, who adds the next word, and so on. Put a pile of commas in the centre of the table; when someone thinks they've reached the end of the fronted adverbial, they grab one, hold it up and shout 'comma!' before going on with the sentence.

Interactive Whiteboard Activity

Use the Online Interactive Whiteboard Activity 'Punctuation' to teach, practise, assess or consolidate the objectives in these units. See details on how to access the activities in the introduction of this book (page 5).

Activity 1 — Repair the sentences by putting commas in the correct places.

a) Running as fast as they could the cats escaped the dogs.

b) My cat likes chasing mice string paper and birds.

c) Although Freya likes lizards she is afraid of snakes.

d) If Samsia answers the next question we will win the quiz.

e) Mr Warren who is our deputy head is great fun

Activity 2 — Can you write a list of five things you would need to camp out for the night? Write your list as a sentence.

a) _____

_____

Can you write a list of five things you would need to visit the beach? Write your list as a sentence.

b) _____

_____

Activity 3 — Can you add extra information to each sentence using an embedded clause?

Laura walked to school.

a) _____

The air was very cold.

b) _____

Skye frowned and said

c) _____

Unit overview

A hyphen is used to join a prefix to a root word, especially if the prefix ends in a vowel and the root word begins with one. A hyphen is also used to join two or more words together in order to avoid confusion over meaning.

Subject knowledge

- A hyphen is a short dash used to connect words or parts of words.
- A hyphen is used after a prefix where it helps to make the meaning clearer. For example:

  co-operate, re-enter, re-elect.

- A hyphen can also make the meaning clearer when linking two words. For example:

  face-to-face, twenty-three, heart-broken.

Using the Pupil Books

Unit 19 in the Skills Builders English Year 5 Grammar and Punctuation Pupil Book gives the children opportunities to practise and consolidate these objectives (see pp42–43). You will also find investigations for challenge.

Possible teaching steps

1. Ask pupils to try reading words without the hyphen, where the prefix ends in a vowel and the root word also begins with one, for example, *reenter, reelect, cooperate.*

2. Give pupils a list of words without hyphens – they rewrite with the hyphens on whiteboards.

3. Demonstrate how missing out a hyphen can change meaning. Ask pupils to explain the difference between *man-eating lion spotted in the local woods* and *man eating lion spotted in the local woods.*

4. Using a range of fiction and non-fiction books, can the children find different examples of where a hyphen is used?

5. Can the children name and give examples of when we use a hyphen. Ask them to write sentences and words to put up on a display.

Interactive Whiteboard Activity

Use the Online Interactive Whiteboard Activity 'Punctuation' to teach, practise, assess or consolidate the objectives in these units. See details on how to access the activities in the introduction of this book (page 5).

Activity 1 Where do you think the hyphen should go in each of these words?

> cooperate   greatgrandmother   soninlaw   thirtytwo
>
> rundown   uptodate   motheaten   heartbroken

Activity 2 Rewrite these sentences adding hyphens to make the sentences clearer.

a) I am thinking of recovering my sofa.

b) France has a 35 hour working week.

c) She won the 100 metre sprint.

d) The sale had rock bottom prices.

e) The man eating tiger ran through the village.

Activity 3 Explain the meaning of each of these words.

a) wide-eyed _____

b) rock-bottom _____

c) light-footed _____

d) hot-headed _____

e) tight-fisted _____

f) flat-footed _____

Unit overview

Apostrophes are used to show where letters are omitted from a word and to show possession.

Subject knowledge

- Omission

  If a letter, or group of letters, is omitted from a word, then an apostrophe shows where they were omitted. For example:

  can't = cannot

  she'll = she will/she shall.

- Possession

  - Words that do not end in 's' (usually singular nouns) have 's added, for example, *Jack's car.*

  - For most names that end in 's', we still add 's, for example, *James's book.*

  - Other words that end in 's' (usually plural nouns) just have an apostrophe added, for example, *the boys' game.*

  - Some names ending in 's' do not add the extra 's', for example, *Socrates' parents.*

- Special note: its and it's

  - These are commonly used incorrectly.

  - The word *it's* is **always** short for *it is* (as in *it's raining*), or in informal speech, for *it has* (as in *it's got six legs*).

  - *Its* **always** means possession. The word *its* means 'belonging to it' (as in *hold its head still while I jump on its back*). It is a possessive pronoun like *his*.

Possible teaching steps

1. Show pupils a picture of a single girl and a group of girls. Hold up some games and say – *These are the girls' games.*

2. Ask the pupils to talk with a partner and decide if you are talking about the singular girl or the group of girls. Collect pupils' ideas and responses. Explain that it is very difficult to tell if it's singular or plural when you say a word, but there is a way to write it that will make it clear.

3. Display the sentence *These are the girls' games.* Ask pupils what is it that shows the ownership of the game? Show them how to cover the apostrophe and what comes after it. The word *girls* should be seen so we know the games belong to more than one girl.

4. Display the sentence *These are the girl's games.* Cover the apostrophe and what comes after it. The word *girl* should be seen now so we know the game belongs to one girl.

5. Repeat with other examples.

6. Share with pupils different words where the apostrophe is used for omission. Can they match the complete word to the omitted word?

Interactive Whiteboard Activity

Use the Online Interactive Whiteboard Activity 'Apostrophes' to teach, practise, assess or consolidate the objectives in these units. See details on how to access the activities in the introduction of this book (page 5).

Activity 1 — Can you work out the contraction addition?

a) did + not = _____

b) _____ + not = couldn't

c) have + not = _____

d) _____ + not = can't

e) _____ + will = he'll

f) _____ + would = I'd

g) should + have = _____

Activity 2 — Tick the sentences that use apostrophes correctly.

a) She can't dance very well. ☐

b) Her work book is full of doodle's. ☐

c) Our school does'nt agree with bullying. ☐

d) He's very fond of reptiles. ☐

Activity 3 — Rewrite each sentence with the apostrophe in the correct place.

a) Seans bag is green' and Hollys bag is red.

_____

b) My aunties house has giant tree's in the garden's

_____

c) The girls' enjoyed playing with the board games.

_____

Unit overview

Words containing the 'ough' letter string are some of the trickiest spellings in English. It is used to spell a number of different sounds.

Subject knowledge

Sounds spelled using 'ough'

Sound	Example
or	ought, bought, thought, nought
off	trough, cough
uff	rough, tough, enough
oe	though, although, dough
oo	through
ow	plough, bough
u	thorough, borough

Using the Pupil Books

Unit 10 in the Skills Builders English Year 5 Spelling and Vocabulary Pupil Book gives the children opportunities to practise and consolidate these objectives (see pp14–15). You will also find investigations for challenge.

Possible teaching steps

1. Explain that the letter string -ough has many different sounds.

2. Ask the pupils to work with a partner and to list any 'ough' words they can find. Ask them to then work out the sound that the 'ough' makes in each word. Collect pupils' ideas and discuss the answers created. If there are any gaps in the subject knowledge sounds, give these to pupils so that they have a full list of all the sounds the 'ough' makes.

3. A great way for pupils to remember information is through song. Share with them 'The ough rap':

   O-u-g-h! O-u-g-h!

   Got to rap! Got to rap!

   We've got to plough and climb this bough,

   And in this borough we'll all be thorough.

   So cough (uh, uh), all cough (uh, uh),

   O-u-g-h! O-u-g-h!

   Got to rap! Got to rap!

   We brought loads 'cos we thought we ought,

   And though, although, you've got a lot of dough,

   You bought us nought, and so we fought.

   O-u-g-h! O-u-g-h!

   Got to rap! Got to rap!

   It's rough and tough and we've really had enough

   And now we're through – it's over to you!

4. Ask pupils to learn the rap and highlight all the 'ough' words. They could teach the rap to younger year groups.

Activity 1

Draw a line to match the words where the same letter string has the same sound.

though	tough
bough	thought
bought	dough
enough	plough

Activity 2

Use a word from below to complete each of the sentences.

brought	through	coughing	rough	ought

a) The boat bobbed up and down on the _____ sea.

b) We need to go _____ the puddle to get to the other side.

c) They _____ to eat their lunch as they are going on a long walk later.

d) We have _____ some fresh fruit for dessert.

e) You have been _____ all night, you may need some medicine.

Activity 3

Write the words with the 'ough' letter string that have these meanings.

a) the past tense of the verb *think* _____

b) used by farmers to turn soil in fields _____

c) a district of a town or city _____

d) raw bread _____

e) strong and hard to break _____

Suffixes: -tious and -cious, -cial and -tial

Unit overview

The spelling of suffixes can often be determined by looking at the root word and other related words.

Subject knowledge

- Suffixes -cious, -tious, -cial and -tial

  - If the root word or related words end with *ce* or *ge*, then the suffixes are usually '-cious' or '-cial', for example, *vice/vicious, finance/financial*

  - If the root word or related words end with *t* or *tion*, then the suffixes are usually '-tious' or '-tial', for example, *ambition/ambitious*.

- Some exceptions:

  - *anxiety/anxious, essence/essential, sequence/sequential, benefit/beneficial, consequence/consequential, preference/preferential*

  - If the root word ends with *ect*, and the spelling stays the same with the suffix, then the suffix is usually '-tious', for example, *infect/infectious*.

  - If the word ends with *ect* and the spelling changes with the suffix, then the suffix is usually '-cious', for example, *suspect/suspicious*.

Possible teaching steps

1. Give pupils a list of words to which the suffixes '-cial' or '-tial' can be added and read the words to check for pronunciation and correct if necessary. An example of the words to use could be: *office, part, artifice, space, provident, confident, finance, resident, race, sacrifice, commerce, judge, evident* and *influence*.

2. Tell pupils that they are going to change the words by using either the suffix '-cial' or '-tial'. Ask them to read the list with a partner, changing the word with the suffix.

3. Pupils say all the words together with the suffix added. Check for any errors. Pupils could check using a dictionary.

4. Can they write down a rule to remind them how and when to add '-cial', or '-tial'?

5. Tell the pupils to work with a partner to spell the new words. Encourage them to use dictionaries to check new spellings. Collect and discuss responses, displaying the correct spellings. Make sure pupils understand that words ending in *ce* and *ge* usually use '-cial' and others use '-tial' but that there are exceptions to the rule.

Using the Pupil Books

Units 11 and 12 in the Skills Builders English Year 5 Spelling and Vocabulary Pupil Book give the children opportunities to practise and consolidate these objectives (see pp18–22). You will also find investigations for challenge.

Interactive Whiteboard Activity

Use the Online Interactive Whiteboard Activity 'Prefixes and suffixes' to teach, practise, assess or consolidate the objectives in these units. See details on how to access the activities in the introduction of this book (page 5).

Activity 1 Write a sentence using each of the words below correctly.

a) sequential

b) beneficial

c) infectious

d) artificial

e) spacious

Activity 2 Write down the meaning of each word first and then a sentence that uses the word correctly.

a) pretentious

_____

b) precious

_____

c) superstitious

_____

d) financial

_____

Activity 3 Draw lines to match the words on the left to their meaning on the right.

Words	Meanings
partial	pleasant tasting
unofficial	incomplete
delicious	existing or occurring at the beginning
initial	not officially authorised or confirmed

Unit overview

The suffixes '-able' and '-ible' can sound similar but there are some rules which can help to distinguish between them and help with spelling.

Subject knowledge

- '-able' suffixes are far more common than '-ible' suffixes.

- The '-able' suffix is used if there is a related word ending in *ation*, for example, *adorable/adoration*, *considerable/consideration*.

- Dropping '-able' generally leaves a recognisable root word, for example, *understandable/ understand*, *considerable/consider*.

- When '-able' is added to a word ending in *ce* or *ge*, the *e* after the *ce* or *ge* must be kept in order to show that the sound is soft, for example, *changeable*, *noticeable*.

Using the Pupil Books

Unit 13 in the Skills Builders English Year 5 Spelling and Vocabulary Pupil Book the children opportunities to practise and consolidate these objectives (see pp21–22). You will also find investigations for challenge.

Possible teaching steps

1. Pupils can write '-able' on one side of their whiteboards and '-ible' on the other. Say aloud a number of words and they have to show if the correct suffix is '-ible' or '-able'. Pupils find a list of words ending with '-ible' and '-able'. They challenge each other to spell the words correctly.

2. Practise changing the endings of root words in order to add '-able', for example:
   - change *y* to *i*
   - drop the final *e*
   - **but** also throw in the exceptions, such as *changeable*.

3. Write a selection of '-able' and '-ible' words on a flip chart, some of which should be incorrect. Can pupils become spelling detectives and work out the correct and incorrect spellings?

Interactive Whiteboard Activity

Use the Online Interactive Whiteboard Activity 'Spelling rules' to teach, practise, assess or consolidate the objectives in these units. See details on how to access the activities in the introduction of this book (page 5).

Activity 1 Write the root word for each of these words with the suffix *able.*

a) agreeable _____

b) disposable _____

c) valuable _____

d) identifiable _____

e) reliable _____

f) forgivable _____

Activity 2 Can you add the suffix *ible* or *able* to each of the underlined words?

a) That chair looks very <u>comfort</u>.

b) Priya is a <u>depend</u> friend and never lets you down.

c) That sounds like a <u>reason</u> idea and change.

d) That bird could be <u>identify</u> if we had a picture of it.

e) The road was not <u>access</u> as a tree had fallen down.

f) The weather is very <u>change</u> at the moment.

g) Do you have an <u>extend</u> paintbrush to reach the ceiling?

h) I think that <u>convert</u> car is the one I will buy.

Activity 3 Decide which suffix is needed to complete these words.

mix accept ador applic aud comfort break consider cred deduc depend
horr imagin imposs manage not permiss profit reason reli remark

Add *ible*	Add *able*

Unit overview

A silent letter is not sounded in a word's pronunciation.

Subject knowledge

- Some reasons for silent letters:
  - They reflect the meaning or origin of the word, for example, *vineyard* relates to *vines*.
  - Sound changes have happened without spelling changes, for example, *gh* used to be pronounced *x* in Middle English, and *k* and *g* were not silent letters.
  - Words are adapted from and reflect the spelling in other languages, for example, *rendezvous*.
  - Some words have been adapted to make them reflect the Latin roots, for example, *debt*.
  - Some speakers pronounce words differently so letters can be silent for some and not others.

- Some letters are silent in some word forms and not others:
  - *Sign* has a silent *g* but it is sounded in *signal*.
  - *Practically* has a silent *a* but it is sounded in *practical*.
  - *Solemn* has a silent *n* but it is sounded in *solemnity*.
  - *Bomb* has a silent *b* but it is sounded in *bombard*.

Possible teaching steps

1. Display a list of words with silent letters. Pupils read the words together to listen for correct pronunciation. Change and correct where necessary.

2. Ask pupils to discuss with a partner what silent letters are. Establish that silent letters are not sounded when the word is spoken.

3. Pupils work with a partner to identify any silent letters in the words. Collect and discuss findings, explaining some of the reasons from the subject knowledge section.

4. Create a display for silent letters that pupils can add to. They could have a spelling challenge where they have to find the longest list of words with silent letters in.

5. Put a list of words with silent syllables on the flip chart. Ask the pupils to read them all out. Then demonstrate how to read them so that you say the silent syllable. What do you notice? Explain that what they are saying is correct, but that, in order to help them spell these words, they need to think about those silent syllables.

Using the Pupil Books

Unit 14 in the Skills Builders English Year 5 Spelling and Vocabulary Pupil Book gives the children opportunities to practise and consolidate these objectives (see pp23–24). You will also find investigations for challenge.

Interactive Whiteboard Activity

Use the Online Interactive Whiteboard Activity 'Silent letters' to teach, practise, assess or consolidate the objectives in these units. See details on how to access the activities in the introduction of this book (page 5).

Activity 1   Can you circle the silent letters in each of these words?

knuckle	wrapper	wrong
wrestle	kneel	chemist
dumb	answer	wrist
knee	know	rhyme
honest	numb	wheat

Activity 2   Add the correct silent letter to the words below.

a) Do you believe in g_osts?

b) There are g_ards at the airport.

c) Leaves change colour in the autum_.

d) Do you _now the ans_er to the question?

e) I have hurt my _rist.

f) There is a small i_land in the middle of the sea.

Activity 3   Choose from the words below to complete the sentences.

honest   writing   doubt   bomb   column

a) Can you add an extra _____ to your table?

b) We have been _____ our story together.

c) I _____ we will finish in time.

d) 'It looks like a _____ has dropped in here!', said Mum.

e) Is that the _____ answer or a lie?

Unit overview

There are rules for knowing when to use double letters in certain situations, but some spellings just have to be learned.

Subject knowledge

- When there is a short vowel sound ending in a single consonant, you double the consonant before adding the suffix, for example, *win/winner, sit/sitting, rot/rotten, stop/stopped.*

- Words with double letters which appear on the word list for Year 5 and Year 6 are: *accommodate, accompany, according, aggressive, apparent, appreciate, attached, committee, communicate, community, correspond, embarrass, exaggerate, excellent, guarantee, harass, immediate, interrupt, marvellous, necessary, occupy, occur, opportunity, profession, programme, recommend, sufficient* and *suggest.*

- Many other words with double letters appear throughout Years 3–6. Some of these words will follow a pattern which will enable pupils to learn them in groups.

Possible teaching steps

1. As with all spellings, some pupils learn visually, by looking at the word, including its shape. Some pupils will draw pictures to remind them of the double letters. Others will say the words and remember them.

2. Pupils may find it helpful to write a list of all the common words with double letters in. The list in the 'Subject knowledge' section could be a suitable start.

3. Can pupils think of rhymes or sayings to remember the words? An example of this could be: *necessary = never eat cakes, eat salad sandwiches and remain young.*

Using the Pupil Books

Unit 15 in the Skills Builders English Year 5 Spelling and Vocabulary Pupil Book gives the children opportunities to practise and consolidate these objectives (see pp25–26). You will also find investigations for challenge.

Activity 1

Decide if these words should have a double or a single c. Add cc or c.

a) o____upy

b) re____ognise

c) a____ommodation

d) o____ur

e) re____ommended

f) ne____essary

Activity 2

Can you add *ing* and *ed* to each of these root words? Remember to change the spelling of the root word where necessary.

Root	Add '-ing'	Add '-ed'
travel		
bake		
equal		
target		
tap		

Activity 3

Cross out the incorrectly spelled word in each question.

a) sitting   showwing   missing   digging

b) smaller   fitter   fixxer   bigger

c) playyer   scammed   planned   scarred

d) smarter   thinner   fater   slimmer

e) attached   programmed   haras   suggest

f) sugest   marvellous   committee   apparent

Unit overview

A prefix is a group of letters added to the beginning of a word that changes or modifies the meaning.

A suffix is a group of letters added to the end of a word that changes or modifies the meaning or changes the tense.

Subject knowledge

- **Prefixes**

  Be aware that some elements, such as 'auto-' or 'bio-' are 'combining forms', not prefixes. A true prefix is followed by a recognisable root word and does not usually change the word class:
  - 're-' (meaning 'again' or 'back')
  - 'dis-'/'un-' (reverse the meaning)
  - 'over-' (meaning 'too much')
  - 'bi-' (meaning 'two')
  - 'out-' (meaning 'more' or 'better than')
  - 'kilo-' (meaning 'thousand')

- **Suffixes**

  Suffixes often change the word class:
  - nouns from verbs: '-ance'; '-tion'; '-er'; '-ing'; '-ment'; '-ure; '-y'
  - adjectives/adverbs from verbs: '-able'/'-ably'; '-ible'/'-ibly'; '-ed'; '-ing'/'-ingly'; '-ive'/'-ively'
  - nouns from nouns: '-ian'; '-ist'
  - adjectives/adverbs from nouns: '-al'/'-ally'; '-ate'/'-ately'; '-ful'/'-fully'; '-ing'/'-ingly'; '-ised'; '-ive'/'-ively'; '-less'/'-lessly'
  - nouns from adjectives: '-ibility'; '-ence'; '-ness'; '-ity'
  - verbs from adjectives: '-ate'; '-en'; '-ify'; '-ise'/'-ize'

Possible teaching steps

1. Give pupils a set of root words and a set of prefixes and suffixes. Test each root word with each prefix and identify any new words that are created and record these words. Repeat using the root words and suffixes. Identify any new words that are created and record these words.

2. Ask pupils to work with a partner and see if they can create any words using a root word with both a prefix and a suffix card. Collect the results and discuss.

3. Can pupils explain what the new words created mean? Use a dictionary to find the new meanings. Can they use these words accurately?

4. Give pupils words and challenge them to add a prefix or a suffix to give an antonym of the original word.

Using the Pupil Books

Unit 17 in the Skills Builders English Year 5 Spelling and Vocabulary Pupil Book gives the children opportunities to practise and consolidate these objectives (see pp29–30). You will also find investigations for challenge.

Activity 1 — Explain the meanings of the following prefixes.

a) re _____

b) bi _____

c) auto _____

d) trans _____

e) super _____

f) tele _____

g) aero _____

Activity 2 — Circle the correct spelling of the word in brackets to complete the sentences.

a) Can you (describe/desccribe) the picture?

b) I am (desparate/desperate) to buy a new pair of shoes.

c) The children had a (disagreement/dissagreement) about their favourite book.

d) The last slice of pizza (disappeared/dissapeared) off the plate.

e) The (decent/discent) down the mountain was very steep and the walkers had to be careful not to fall.

f) The author had to (review/reeview) the book before it was published.

Unit overview

The word list for Year 5 can be found in both of the Skills Builders Teacher's Guide for Year 5 and Skills Builders Teacher's Guide for Year 6.

Subject knowledge

- There are words that have been identified for Year 5 pupils to learn.
  - Many root words simply need to be learned, but once they are learned, and the rules and guidance for adding prefixes and suffixes are known, many longer words can be spelled correctly, for example: *business* (busy + -ness, with the 'y' of *busy* changed to 'i' according to the rule) and *disappear* (just add *dis-* to *appear*). Many of the words can be used for practice in adding suffixes.

Word list for Year 5

Please visit www.risingstars-uk.com to find a full copy of the Year 5 word list.

Possible teaching steps

1. Pupils will need to learn to spell each of these words and be able to add s, prefixes and suffixes accurately.

2. Prepare a set of flashcards with the Year 5 words on. Distribute the words to pupils in groups and ask them to sort the words they have been given. Pupils can choose their own criteria and then explain this to another group.

3. Pupils choose a word each and sit in a circle. Choose a story style and start the story, and each pupil adds a sentence to the story using the word on their card.

4. Once the children can spell all of these words add prefixes and suffixes to the words and think about the rules for adding the prefixes and suffixes.

Using the Pupil Books

Unit 20 in the Skills Builders English Year 5 Spelling and Vocabulary Pupil Book gives the children opportunities to practise and consolidate these objectives (see pp35–36). You will also find investigations for challenge.

Activity 1 — Underline the words that are spelled correctly.

a) goverment   govenment   government

b) develop   deveip   develap

c) laishur   leisure   lesure

d) eggistence   existence   egistence

e) interfere   interfear   intafere

Activity 2 — Practise writing and spelling the following words.

	Look Cover Say Check
accommodate	
accompany	
according	
achieve	
aggressive	
amateur	
ancient	

Activity 3 — Write a sentence including the following words.

a) accommodate _____

b) controversy _____

c) mischievous _____

d) awkward _____

e) interrupted _____

f) apparent _____

g) curiosity _____

h) occupy _____

Unit overview

Year 5 pupils need to know how to use both a dictionary and a thesaurus.

Subject knowledge

- Year 5 pupils are expected to:
  - use a dictionary to check the spelling and meanings of words
  - use the first three or four letters of a word to check spelling, meaning or both of these in a dictionary
  - use a thesaurus to find different words to make their writing interesting.

Using the Pupil Books

Unit 21 in the Skills Builders English Year 5 Spelling and Vocabulary Pupil Book gives the children opportunities to practise and consolidate these objectives (see pp37–38). You will also find investigations for challenge.

Possible teaching steps

1. Make sure your class gets into the habit of actually checking unknown spellings in a dictionary, not leaving words as their own phonetic transcription.

2. Have dictionary races. Reveal differentiated words (which are deliberately misspelled at the end) on the board and pairs race to find and correct each one using their dictionaries, giving the page number to prove they've looked it up. You could also use this to introduce new topic vocabulary, although not all the vocabulary you might want to include will be in smaller dictionaries!

3. To avoid pupils getting bogged down with a spelling during independent writing time, suggest they have a go at it, then highlight the word and move on. Allow five minutes at the end of the session/during registration for checking the correct spelling in their dictionary.

4. Have a weekly synonym challenge. Pick a word at random from your marking or a guided reading text and ask the class to find as many alternatives as they can, using a thesaurus.

5. Dedicate a corner of your VCOP wall to synonyms for common overused words (e.g. *mad/bad/sad*) and remind pupils to look there when they're writing. This is great for developing reporting verbs in dialogue, for example, *How many ways can we avoid saying 'said'?*

6. Use a thesaurus in combination with a dictionary, so pupils find meanings for new words/phrases as well. Pupils often use words from the thesaurus inappropriately, because they're not aware that the meaning isn't exactly the same as the word they're trying to replace.

7. When marking, highlight an unambitious word choice in their work, to be upgraded using a thesaurus during improvement time. Use the same highlighter colour every time, so your class knows that purple, for example, means 'Use a thesaurus to make this word better please'.

Activity 1

Use a dictionary to check if the spelling of these words is correct. If it is not, write the correct spelling next to the incorrect word.

a) atractive _____

b) teecher _____

c) stewdant _____

d) beutiful _____

e) undagrownd _____

f) elektrisitie _____

g) unyusuwal _____

Activity 2

Some words have very similar meanings. You can use a dictionary to discover how they are different.

Look up the words below in a dictionary and write down what is slightly different about each of them.

a) hill   peak   mountain   fell

_____

b) street   path   lane   road

_____

c) horror   fright   terror   fear

_____

Activity 3

Can you use a thesaurus to find different words which mean the same or are similar to the following words?

Write the words that you find next to each.

happy   **nice**

walk   **sad**

Unit overview

An idiom is a word or phrase that means something completely different from the word or words it is made up of. The meanings of idiom have little or no relation to the literal meanings of their counterparts, but they make sense because they are familiar expressions.

Idioms are often metaphorical expressions. Every language has its own idioms. Idioms are used in informal speech and writing.

Subject knowledge

- **Examples of literal meanings of idioms**

Idiom	Literal meaning	Intended meaning
Raining cats and dogs	Cats and dogs are falling from the sky	Raining very heavily
Break a leg	Break a bone in your leg	Do your best/good luck
Face the music	Look to where the music is being played	Face up to the consequences of your actions
Get up and go	Stand up and leave the room	Energy
At the eleventh hour	At eleven o'clock	At the last minute

- **Other idioms**
  - A blessing in disguise = something good that isn't recognised as good at the start.
  - Add fuel to the fire = make a bad situation worse.
  - Back to square one = having to start all over again.
  - Crack someone up = make someone laugh.

Possible teaching steps

1. Do pupils know any idioms and which ones have they heard?

2. Give pupils a list of familiar idioms. Can they match the idiom to the intended meaning?

3. Can pupils create their own idioms and make a poster to represent their intended meanings?

4. Create a class library of the idioms. Each pupil writes one idiom on a piece of card and adds the meaning to it. Display the cards around the room and then add them to the class library to use.

5. Give the pupils a selection of idioms to discuss. Come up with a literal meaning for each one, which they could sketch a picture of. Explain any meanings that they know and try to work out any that they don't. What are the clues?

Using the Pupil Books

Unit 22 in the Skills Builders English Year 5 Spelling and Vocabulary Pupil Book gives the children opportunities to practise and consolidate these objectives (see pp39–40). You will also find investigations for challenge.

Interactive Whiteboard Activity

Use the Online Interactive Whiteboard Activity 'Build a description' to teach, practise, assess or consolidate the objectives in these units. See details on how to access the activities in the introduction of this book (page 5).

Activity 1   Draw a line to match each idiom to its meaning.

believe it or not
break a leg
dawn till dusk
nuts and bolts
strike a balance
down to earth

realistic
all day long
you might not believe this but…
have a good balance of
details
good luck

Activity 2   Use each of the idioms from Activity 1 to create your own sentences.

a) _____

_____

b) _____

_____

c) _____

_____

d) _____

_____

e) _____

_____

f) _____

_____

Unit overview

Year 5 pupils should understand that antonyms are words that mean the opposite.

Subject knowledge

- Antonyms can be made using the prefixes 'anti-', 'un-', 'in-', 'im-', 'il-', 'non-' and 'dis-', for example, *unbelievable*, *indirect*, *illegal*, *disappoint*.

- Antonyms can be made using the suffixes '-ful' and '-less', for example, *hopeful/hopeless*, *careful/careless*.

- Antonyms can be completely different words, for example, *delicious/revolting*, *ugly/beautiful*.

Using the Pupil Books

Unit 23 in the Skills Builders English Year 5 Spelling and Vocabulary Pupil Book gives the children opportunities to practise and consolidate these objectives (see pp41–42). You will also find investigations for challenge.

Possible teaching steps

1. Pupils need to understand that an antonym is a word that has the opposite meaning. They can often be made by using a negative prefix.

2. Give pupils a selection of words and ask them to write them on a whiteboard. Then they work in pairs to use a negative prefix to create an antonym.

3. Give pupils part of a story. Ask them to find as many words as they can to change to an antonym. What has happened to the meaning of the story?

4. Focus on shades of meanings. Collect a set of synonyms and find an antonym for each, for example, *freezing, cold, cool = roasting, hot, warm; large, huge, gigantic = small, tiny, miniscule*.

Interactive Whiteboard Activity

Use the Online Interactive Whiteboard Activity 'Build a description' to teach, practise, assess or consolidate the objectives in these units. See details on how to access the activities in the introduction of this book (page 5).

Activity 1   Rewrite each sentence, replacing one word in each with an *antonym* to change the meaning.

a) 'I love ice-cream!' squealed Hannah.

_____

b) 'Where are you going?' said Mohammed.

_____

c) 'Bring a coat,' ordered Mum.

_____

d) 'We need to hurry,' yelled the attendant.

_____

Activity 2   Change the meaning of these sentences by replacing the underlined words with antonyms.

1. The <u>kind</u>, <u>old</u> lady <u>walked</u> <u>slowly</u> down the street.

2. The <u>fierce</u> lion roared at the <u>naughty</u> children.

3. The <u>brave</u>, <u>intelligent</u> knight attacked the <u>stupid</u> dragon.

4. The <u>evil</u>, <u>old</u> wizard cast a <u>horrible</u> spell on the <u>beautiful</u>, <u>young</u> princess.

5. The <u>angry</u> teacher <u>shouted</u> <u>loudly</u> at the naughty children.

Activity 3   Fill in the missing words, which have opposite meanings, to complete the sentences.

a) The corridor was _____ but the river was _____.

b) The hare was _____ and the tortoise was _____.

c) Snow is _____ but a Summer's day is _____.

d) A horn is _____ but a library is _____.

Answers

Unit Number	Unit Heading	Activity Number	Answers
1	Word class – nouns, verbs, conjunctions, pronouns, adverbs, prepositions and determiners	1	a) adjective b) verb c) noun d) verb
		2	a) a b) an c) an d) a e) an f) a g) an h) an
		3	a) a the b) an a the c) the a the d) the
2	Modal verbs	1	a) could b) will c) might d) could e) will f) could
		2	Any modal verb that makes sense, for example: a) They shall come to the party tomorrow. b) Maria might not be able to sing at the concert as she has lost her voice. c) Jamie should win the race if he tries his best. d) It could rain tomorrow just as the weather forecast says. e) The school should open tomorrow for the children.
		3	a) certain b) certain c) impossible d) possible e) certain
3	Clauses and phrases	1	Answers may vary but should show an understanding of what a subordinate clause is e.g. a) if it is dry b) as it's a rainy day c) to eat with my drink d) you have been running for a while e) to show it's correct f) if the weather forecast is correct
		2	a) As soon as the meat was eaten, <u>the lions strolled away</u>. b) <u>I sent a letter</u> that arrived a week late. c) <u>My sister</u>, who lives with me, <u>loves dogs</u>. d) <u>Do you know the boy</u> who is wearing the football shirts? e) <u>I ate the fruit</u> that was in the fruit bowl. f) <u>I really enjoyed the new film</u> that we watched last night.
		3	a) so b) but c) or d) yet
4	Expanded noun phrases	1	The <u>fast and skilful footballer</u> scored the <u>first magnificent goal</u>. It turned out that this <u>amazing goal</u> was the only one of the <u>damp and boring game of football</u>. The <u>angry crowd</u> shouted and booed loudly at their <u>usually fantastic team</u>. After the match the <u>long-standing manager</u> was sacked and they replaced him with a <u>new and improved one</u>. The <u>fanatical fans</u> hope that this <u>new manager</u> will win the <u>all important trophy</u> at the end of the season.
		2	a) Pre =fresh, currant Post = looked and b) Pre = old, thoughtful Post = stood and c) Pre = fast, red Post = which could beat d) Pre = new, state-of-the-art Post = caught the wind and
		3	Have you seen my new bicycle seat? Please pass me the packet of crisps.
		4	Large bikes are not allowed on the playground. Jo took her sister's new sparkly dress.

58

5	Relative pronouns	1	a) who b) who c) where d) which e) who f) which
		2	a) Chocolate, which contains 'feel good' chemicals, originates in South America. b) The Queen, who owns several castles, is one of the richest women in the world. c) At 8 o'clock last night, when I had finished my homework, I went to bed. d) Phillip Pullman, who wrote *Clockwork*, is my favourite writer. e) Ostriches, that are the world's largest birds, live in Africa. f) We are having fishcakes, which I hate, for tea.
		3	a) who b) which c) whose d) which
6	Paragraphs and linked ideas across paragraphs	1	b, d, a, c
		2	a) Later, she could see the tramps. b) She looked up, to check if the old tenement blocks were about to fall down on her. c) Anna hated walking through Southside. d) The oldies never went out at dusk.
		3	Answers will vary.
7	Adverbials and fronted adverbials (revision from Year 3 and 4)	1	a) very quickly down the road. b) loudly as she was very sleepy. c) quickly as I was hungry. d) quickly and broke the window. e) extremely
		2	a) over the wall. b) for the family to live in. c) heavily and created lots of puddles. d) as it's my friends birthday.
		3	a) It is a hot day so b) My friends were coming over so c) There was a thunderstorm, d) It is a Bank Holiday so e) I dropped the ball but f) We had baked a cake so
8	Present perfect form and past perfect tense	1	a) watched b) had, ate c) knocked d) cried, fell
		2	c), e)
		3	a) The lions <u>roar</u> loudly in the jungle. (present) b) Danielle <u>had</u> her own pony for nine years. (past) c) It has <u>been</u> a great week as it <u>was</u> my birthday. (past) d) Tom <u>ate</u> his lunch with his friends. (past) e) The ice <u>is</u> melting in the summer sun. (present) f) The baby <u>is</u> walking for the first time. (present)
9	Subject and verb agreement	1	a) was → were b) slides → slide c) was → were d) are → is e) rides → rode
		2	a) talk b) talk c) talk d) talk e) talk
		3	a) shout b) goes c) fall d) are e) are
10	'I' and 'me'	1	a) me b) I c) me d) me e) me f) I
		2	a), e)
		3	If you and <u>I</u> were travelling to Manchester, <u>I</u> would travel on a train. It would be easier for Sandra and <u>me</u> to drive as <u>I</u> have lots of luggage to take with <u>me</u>. When we get there, Sandra and <u>I</u> will visit the main attractions. <u>I</u> especially like the old buildings. Sandra and <u>I</u> are going to have a wonderful trip!

11	Changing nouns or adjectives into verbs using suffixes -ate, -ise, -ify, -en	1	a) pollinate b) notify c) dramatise d) authorise e) light Sentences will vary.
		2	a) solidify b) simplify c) legalise d) sweeten e) activate Sentences will vary.
		3	a) terrify b) advertise c) classify
12	Using and spelling verb prefixes dis-, de-, mis-, over-, re- and pre-	1	dis – reverse the meaning de – opposite mis – wrongly over – too much re – again pre – before
		2	<table><tr><th>Prefix</th><th>Root word</th><th>Meaning</th></tr><tr><td>De</td><td>Throne</td><td>fill too much</td></tr><tr><td>Over</td><td>Rail</td><td>remove from a throne</td></tr><tr><td>Dis</td><td>Build</td><td>show lack of respect</td></tr><tr><td>Re</td><td>Respect</td><td>build again</td></tr><tr><td>Mis</td><td>Fill</td><td>cause a train to leave the track</td></tr><tr><td>de</td><td>Take</td><td>get something wrong</td></tr></table>
		3	a) dis- b) mis- c) mis- d) un- e) dis- f) over-
13	Brackets, dashes and commas to indicate parenthesis	1	a) David talks all the time (he never stops) and it drives us all mad. b) My dog has had a litter of puppies (three in total) and they are all white. c) My favourite book is Cinderella (I only like traditional tales). d) Megan (who has been practising her somersaults) will be entering the competition today. e) Goats (although renowned for eating almost anything) mostly eat grass, bushes and leaves. f) The teacher (who enjoyed singing) started a choir at her school.
		2	Any answers that make sense, for example: a) which is my sister's b) in Chester c) as they have a lot of teeth d) with cream and marshmallows
		3	a) a Ford Fiesta b) who is called Mr Taylor c) which is next to the basketbal d) he's called Eric e) the kind with the flip screen f) 20 metres high
14	Commas to clarify meaning and avoid ambiguity	1	a) Running as fast as they could, the cats escaped the dogs. b) My cat likes chasing mice, string, paper and birds. c) Although Freya likes lizards, she is afraid of snakes. d) If Samsia answers the next question, we will win the quiz. e) Mr Warren, who is our deputy head, is great fun.
		2	Any answers that make sense, for example: a) rucksack, fire, torch, first aid kit and a tent b) costume, bucket, spade, sun cream and a hat

		3	Any answers that make sense, for example: a) who was eight years old b) in Manchester c) What is it?
15	Hyphens	1	co-operate, great-grandmother, son-in-law, thirty-two, run-down, up-to-date, moth-eaten, heart-broken
		2	a) I am thinking of re-covering my sofa. b) France has a 35-hour working week. c) She won the 100-metre sprint. d) The sale had rock-bottom prices. e) The man-eating tiger ran through the village.
		3	a) surprised b) down on your luck c) walks gently d) has a short temper e) doesn't like to spend money f) walk in a heavy way
16	Apostrophes	1	a) didn't b) could c) haven't d) can e) he f) I g) should've h) shouldn't i) have
		2	a), d)
		3	a) Sean's bag is green and Holly's bag is red. b) My auntie's house has giant trees in the gardens. c) The girls enjoyed playing with the board games.
17	Letter string 'ough'	1	though - dough bough - plough bought - thought enough - tough
		2	a) rough b) through c) ought d) brought e) coughing
		3	a) thought b) plough c) borough d) dough e) tough
18	Suffixes tious and cious, cial and tial	1	Answers will vary.
		2	a) thinks they are much better than the others b) very important and valuable c) having or showing a belief in superstitions d) the cost of something
		3	partial – incomplete unofficial – not officially authorized or comfirmed delicious – pleasant tasting initial – existing or occurring at the beginning
19	Suffixes able and ible	1	a) agree b) dispose c) value d) identify e) rely f) forgive
		2	a) comfortable b) dependable c) reasonable d) identifiable e) accessible f) changeable g) extendable h) convertible
		3	Mixable, acceptable, adorable, applicable, audible, comfortable, breakable, considerable, credible, deducible, dependable, horrible, imaginable, impossible, manageable, notable, permissible, profitable, reasonable, reliable, remarkable

20	Silent letters	1	Ⓚnuckle Ⓦrapper Ⓦrong Ⓦresⓣle Ⓚneel cⒽemist dumⒷ ansⓌer Ⓦrist Ⓚnee Ⓚnow rⒽyme Ⓗonest numⒷ wⒽeat
		2	a) h b) u c) n d) k e) w f) s
		3	a) column b) writing c) doubt d) bomb e) honest
21	Double letters	1	a) occupy b) recongnise c) accommodate d) occur e) recommended f) necessary
		2	travelling/travelled baking/baked equalling/equalled target/targeted
		3	a) showing b) fixer c) player d) fatter e) harass f) suggest
22	Adding prefixes and suffixes	1	a) again b) two c) self d) across e) greater f) carry g) air
		2	a) describe b) desperate c) disagreement d) disappeared e) decent f) review
23	Statutory word list	1	a) government b) develop c) leisure d) existence e) interfere
		2	Check the children have spelled the words correctly.
		3	Any answers which are appropriate e.g. a) The hotel will accommodate you. b) The game was full of controversy. c) The children were very mischievous. d) The puzzle was very awkward. e) The children interrupted the teacher. f) Is it apparent that the sky is blue? g) The children were full of curiosity about the mysterious box. h) The birds will occupy the bird box soon.
24	Using a dictionary and thesaurus	1	a) attractive b) teacher c) student d) beautiful e) underground f) electricity g) unusual
		2	Check for understanding.
		3	happy – contented, cheerful, merry, jovial walk – stroll, saunter, amble, trudge sad – sorrow, regretful, downcast, miserable nice – pleasant, delightful, satisfying, likable

25	Idioms	1	Believe it or not — You might not believe this but… Break a leg — Good luck Dawn till dusk — All day long Nuts and bolts — Details Strike a balance — Have a good balance of Down to earth — Realistic
		2	Answers will vary.
26	Antonyms	1	Answers will vary.
		2	Answers will vary.
		3	a) narrow/wide b) fast/slow c) cold/hot d) loud/quiet